# Slime Queen

### Journey of a Nine Year Old Entrepreneur

 Friesenpress

Suite 300 - 990 Fort St
Victoria, BC, V8V 3K2
Canada

www.friesenpress.com

**Copyright © 2019 by Alayna Ffrench**
First Edition — 2019

All rights reserved.

No part of this publication may be reproduced in any form, or by any means, electronic or mechanical, including photocopying, recording, or any information browsing, storage, or retrieval system, without permission in writing from FriesenPress.

ISBN
978-1-5255-5886-3 (Hardcover)
978-1-5255-5887-0 (Paperback)
978-1-5255-5888-7 (eBook)

1. JUVENILE NONFICTION, BUSINESS & ECONOMICS

Distributed to the trade by The Ingram Book Company

# Slime Queen

## Journey of a Nine Year Old Entrepreneur

By Alayna Ffrench

# Chapter One: Starting My First Business

Hi, my name is Alayna Ffrench. I'm nine years old and I have a deep passion for being successful.

This is my journey and I want to share my ups and downs with you. There are only so many businesses you can create out of thin air as a kid. I tried everything. First I tried making my own baby doll food using baking soda and food coloring. I packaged the baby food in little folded pieces of paper and I drew a picture of the food that was inside. I had green veggie, banana apple, and blueberry flavours. I even listed the ingredients on the back and made instructions for how to mix the ingredients together. This baby food idea was simple, easy, and affordable, but there was one problem: not everyone was into baby food and had a doll that could consume it.

I had so many ideas and so little resources that I was starting to get frustrated. I thought of making my own dolls but getting the moulds and silicone was too expensive plus I'd have to paint and mould the dolls by hand, which I'd be better at when I'm older. I also tried to start my own summer camp in my complex to get kids to be active and play games, but some kids didn't get along or want pay the $5 fee for expenses. To make matters worse, I didn't have enough money supplies or enough participants.

So get this: I was making slime one day and I realized how much I actually love slime. If you didn't know, slime is a gooey substance that never gets old but is shapable like dough so you can knead it, squeeze it, roll it up, and poke at it... very entertaining!

Then I had a crazy idea. I knew how I was going to become a nine year old entrepreneur. I was going to start my own slime business! I knew it was going to be challenging but I was very dedicated and committed to seeing my hard work pay off.

This is where my journey begins:

First off, I had to tell my mom my crazy idea. She was on board and we rushed to the dollar store to get the magical supplies. My list of supplies:
- white school glue
- multi-colored glitter
- small plastic water-proof containers with lids (4oz)
- eye contact lens solution with boric acid (activator)
- labels to brand my product
- stickers for presentation

When I got back home, I organized all of my supplies, got a bowl, and got straight to mixing. I also had to work on a flyer to promote my epic slime creations. My personal assistant (Mom) was in charge of getting copies and packaging. LOL.

I needed to learn how to make slime of high quality. After a few failed attempts of making slime with my cousin Shanaya, we finally realized that just the right amount of glue, activator, and baking soda can make the most amazing slime. I did some research and started watching tutorials as I was very desperate to get my product made to perfection. My friends and I came together and each of us brought some ingredients and we combined them all and shared our ideas. We made just enough slime to go around. We were super impressed with our success. Shanaya helped me a lot because she was super motivated to support me.

A container of small slime (any variety) was $2.00. I added stickers and contact information to my packages. I decided to call my business "Slime Therapy Inc." because slime helps me calm down and destress, and it's therapeutic. When I'm making slime it puts me in a positive mood and I get time to myself to be creative and productive.

As I was packaging my amazing slime creations for my friends at school, I was feeling so proud of myself. I knew my slime would be in demand because my friends always talk about slime but it seems their parents are super busy and never had time to go to the stores and pick up slime.

Plus, store bought slime is not as good quality as homemade slime. What kid doesn't want to knead and twist and stretch and squeeze ooey-gooey slime between their hands?

# Chapter Two: Launching My Product

The next day I was armed and dangerous with my slime and receipt books. Nothing could stop this entrepreneurial spirit. I had a handy lil chest that I would use to collect money, receipts, and orders.

When I got to school, the first thing I did was set up shop at my desk. I had my flyers out on display and my slime too. Then I planned to strategically sell my slime and get the word out at first break. I asked my friend to hand out the most amazing, decorative, wonderful, and most vibrant posters in the world (or just the school lol). Everyone began crowding me saying " What types of slime do you have," "Great deal," and "What sizes do you have?" At that moment I felt great, on top of the world, because I was about to reveal my creations to the whole school. I couldn't believe how many of my peers were actually interested in purchasing slime. My hard work was paying off. Yaaaaaayyyyyyyyy!

Alayna Ffrench

### Dear Unicorn Friend,

Yesterday was amazing. I sold so much slime; I'm so impressed with myself. It was hard work and very challenging but I got my first orders completed, packaged, and delivered on time. Well I still have more orders... but I have to get ready for school. I hope my peers at school (mostly grade 4s) can be patient. "Alayna, calm down, the customers will still buy their slimes tomorrow... right? You shouldn't worry, you'll be okay," my inner unicorn would say. My peers are depending on me, I have to do exactly what I said I was going to do and that's produce slime on time if I want people to buy slime and my business to be successful. OH NO! It's 8:40 a.m. I gotta go catch my school bus! Gotta fly!

**Business Tip #1: Understand supply and demand, which means always make sure you have your product ready to go. When the customers demand it, you supply it! That's an important step towards your business' success.**

# Chapter Three: My First Mistake

Okay, I'm at school and I'm just going to deal with slime orders at break hoping it will go smoothly. All the people in my class who ordered slime are saying, "We brought our money can we get our slimes when the bell rings?" and I said, "Okay no problem," with an optimistic tone; even though I didn't bring most of their slimes because I was so overwhelmed with orders I couldn't keep up. The lunch bell rang and it was time to get our lunches. I had an amazing lunch packed and couldn't wait to eat it; I was starving. Disastrously, all the kids who wanted their slimes were crowding me yelling, **"We want our slimes, we brought the money, did you bring them?"** I nervously replied, "I'll be with you in just a moment." I tried to eat my lunch in peace but noooo that wasn't an option; they wanted their precious slime and they wanted it ASAP! I could sense their frustration, but what could I do? I was behind on my orders and they were very mad and almost in tears. But I realized as the chaos was erupting around me that I need to take my time and just breathe. I promised my customers that I would bring their slime in the next day... but I couldn't complete orders on time. I learned a valuable lesson, Instead I will plan ahead, only take as many orders as I can handle and hire helpers (light bulb moment).

    I woke up the next day at 7 a.m. and went straight to getting ready for school. I made my lunch and ate a healthy breakfast wrap with eggs, spinach, peppers, and chicken. My mom says my brain needs nutrients. Of course, I gotta dress the part of an entrepreneur, so I chose to wear black slacks, my fancy blouse, and a silk scarf with royal blue violets; business woman coming through. Just so happens that ever since I was four years old and could dress myself, I had a natural instinct for creating fashion forward outfits that match from head to toe. I believe my ideas stem from my Aunt Tara's polished appearance. I used to watch her lay her outfits on the bed to make sure they were just right. I also have very thick curly hair, so I always spray it with conditioner and brush it out. I put it up in a nice high ponytail and braided it down to the left side and topped it off with a pink fluffy bow that fits my signature look for now.

**Business Tip #2: Dress the part.** Another way to lead your business into success is to be as professional as you can. People will take you more seriously and show more interest in your business and you will attract the right people if you dress professionally. How you look and treat yourself is how people will treat you.

# Chapter Four: Receipts Are a Must

Every morning before school I like to get organized. I begin by packing my backpack. Packing my backpack is easy and fun because it has lots of pockets and space, plus it's super glam. My school bag/business bag is light purple with gold zippers and accents. It also has a pink heart on the front; my mom got it from Amazon, her favorite place to shop.

My awesome backpack contains:
1. Agenda
2. Lunch & water bottle
3. Completed homework pages
4. Slime (of course)
5. Chapstick
6. Pencil case
7. Body mist
8. Satin burgundy mittens
9. Navy blue ear warmers

10. Pink hat with cheetah print and a vibrant yellow pom-pom on top

Conveniently, my school bus picks me up in front of my house, so pretty much valet style. Today, I pretend it's a black limo and I have a seat all to myself, which is great. It only takes five minutes to get to school, and when I arrived, my friends compliment my hair, style and ask me if my mom picked out my outfit lol she didn't. It's freezing outside and the wind is turning my cheeks rosy red and I can't wait to get inside where I can set up my desk so my peers can hand in their orders. I keep everything well organized in my handy little chest; luckily it has a lock on it. I always give my customers a receipt for their order

Here's how I set up my receipts:

**Date:** November 18 **Name:** Geneva
**Order Description:**
One small fluffy cloud and one medium unicorn sparkle
**Total cost:** $7.00 paid

With a description of the variety, for example: "Fluffy Cloud, that's my best seller! The reason I make different varieties of slime is because different people like different colors, consistencies, and I like to embrace my customers' preferences.

# Chapter Five: Embrace Your Inner Cookie Mold

Let your personality shine like a rainbow. Never be afraid to be you. Believe in yourself just the way I believe in unicorns. Expressing your ideas and enthusiasm is so powerful and contagious. Keep your energy positive and optimistic and see the difference in people's responses to you.

**Business Tip #3: Get to know your customer. Asking them what exactly they like about your product . I ask color slime they prefer and I always have a variety to choose from. Also, ask questions about what they might like. For instance, my mom likes diamonds, so I created a slime for her with diamonds called Luxury Slime. These little hints can help with future ideas for sales.**

Alayna Ffrench

The great thing about slime is that it's gooey so you can add charms that fit every personality or occasion. The charms are made like mini cupcakes, cookies, candy, unicorn, hearts, four leaf clovers, Easter eggs, Christmas trees, and so on.

By embracing my **inner cookie mold**, I have single-handedly figured out how to connect with my customers on a deeper level. By understanding and analyzing their personalities, I have mastered the art of selling slime efficiently and effectively.

For instance, Chloe is a very nice, enthusiastic girl who is obsessed with slime, and she also loves bright colors and glitter. Then there's Sarah; she loves cupcakes, rainbows, and poopsey unicorn surprise, plus she's very kind and always includes people. Sarah likes the Fruit Slice Slime, which I offer on my order form, and she ordered 10. I sold out in one day! One thing about Sarah is that she loves new and exciting things. When we first met, she gave me a huge hug and we talked about slime for hours.

**Business Tip #4: Hire employees that shine bright like stars. Look for optimistic, friendly, caring, and enthusiastic people who are supportive and get the job done right. These key employees will make or break your business.**

*Slime Queen*

My friend Lucy volunteers to help me out with my slime business. She has a big personality; she offered to hand out my slime posters and helped to promote my business by yelling out "Get your slime here everyone!" and "Slime for $2, one week only!" She's a very helpful employee; she loves to try new things and she always helps me come up with new ideas. She's very kind and approachable and being a sweet person helps when it comes to selling! I don't know what I'd do without her. When I'm in a rush, Lucy helps the customers fill out their order forms. She gets receipts done, she's there to meet my customers at the green box, and when I'm not there, Lucy kindly updates my customers on orders. She delivers slime on time and she's very trustworthy and dependable.

Dear Unicorn Diary,

"Another day, another dollar" as my Uncle Bronson use to say. I counted my stash and added up all the receipts, and my total sales for the week were $50.00 to be exact. I'm pretty impressed with myself… I'm a natural born hustler. I feel on top of the world, like a flying unicorn dabbing in the sky LOL. I am going to play with my slime and package my new orders and get them ready for school tomorrow. Supply and demand, am I right?"

# Chapter Six: Rules for Myself

These are the 9 simple rules I always try to follow:

#1 Have a good attitude

#2 Always make sure to love myself and not push myself too hard

#3 Have fun, appreciate the little moments, and enjoy the process of being creative

#4 Live in the moment

#5 Be myself

#6 Live my passion and dreams

#7 Be thankful

#8 Inspire those around me to always strive to reach their greatest potential

#9 No matter what people say, don't get discouraged. I just tell myself "You can do it!"

#10 Get in your warm and fuzzy place, cherish life!

Alayna FFrench signing off.

# Chapter Seven: My Hobbies

It's a new day, the sun is shining; I am about to meditate and take deep breaths. Every day I like to pull out a book and read the *Baby-Sitters Club* novels, but today my quiet time is limited. My lil brother and sister love to knock on my door because they want to go on my tablet, play with my dolls, and touch everything, omg. They want to mess up all my important papers and files, like a business woman needs her space! I also like to do some finger knitting, making headbands and blankets for my baby doll. I just got a new Luvabeau doll that says a lot of cute phrases and moves on its own, goes to sleep, blinks. and plays peek-a-boo. I call my doll L'il Tyler; having him makes me feel like an experienced independent mother. I know what these hard working mothers go through, there's just one catch: L'il Tyler has an off switch. I also love to play with my squishies because sometimes it's cute to play house and pretend I have a cute happy family of squishies. The pink fox I call Foxy; she gets the name for being so colorful. She loves going to tea parties, birthday parties, and sleep overs. The two pink poop emojis I call the Pinky-Winky twins; they love to hang out in their unicorn house with their brother and they love gardening. They love school and education, they love people, and they live in unicorn village. I also have a pink ice cream sundae squishy I call Sunday Salon Girl; she's a girly-girl/diva who only goes to the salon on Sundays.

    I also like to play my recorder. My favorite to play is *Hot Cross Buns*. I also made a song up called *Magical Jasmine* because it was inspired by the music from the movie *Aladdin*. I also took sewing lessons and made a beautiful purple and yellow quilt with butterflies on it. I never knew how much detailed work went into making a professional quilt. I love to draw, do sketches from my books, and I create characters. Animals are fun to draw, especially horses. I also love to draw angels. I draw pictures of myself as a successful business woman walking to my office in Paris. Paris really inspires me because I love the Eiffel Tower, the cafes, the French language, and they do a lot of business there like fashion designing; Paris is my dream destination. Some day when I'm older I will move there!

# Chapter Eight: Squishie Meltdown, Market Test

Okay so I have expanded my horizons. My mom bought me a set of squishies and I asked her how much they cost. She said "$20 for 5 squishies," so I divided 20 by 5 which equals $4 per squishie, and I decided to do a practice run and test the market. I brought my squishies to school to see if my peers were interested. OMG, you don't even know. EVERYONE was literally surrounding me asking in excited voices, "What is that Alayna? How much is it? Are they scented?" My loyal customers were begging to touch them and squeeze them and I said "First come, first serve! They are for sale, $5 each." They were asking me if this was a one day thing and I said, "I can sell them once or twice a week." By the time the last bell rang they were all sold. My peers were ecstatic with joy and I was thinking that I should have brought more. I was in a very unique position because no one else brought squishies to school especially for sale so that meant I was their #1 supplier. BOOOOYEAH!

My ideas are endless! As I grow older, I can't stop thinking about all the new inventions and things I can make, including new and improved slime recipes, homemade squishies, strawberry scented putty, and more stress relieving ideas for girls and boys. I have inspired a lot of people to make their own business and become an entrepreneur.

There's this in my class named Zain who decided to make his own business because I inspired him as one of my employees—my accountant to be exact. He helped me with pricing and he was very helpful; he learned a lot about business from his mom. So he decided to create his own game with characters and it came with mini cars and figurines. But one day something happened that wasn't so great: five people who ordered his game decided after he went to all the trouble of making their orders that it wasn't worth the money of $5 for the kit which included two cars, one figurine, and six playing cards (they could also purchase items separately: $2 for one car, $4 for two figurines, and $3 for five cards). Zain was very upset when he brought the kit to his customers and they turned their backs on him, ignored him, and kept their money. He was soo disappointed because he couldn't pay his employees who worked very hard to make the figurines, flyers, and kits. Zain didn't want to make a scene and he put the stuff back in his bag and took his product back home. I felt so bad for him that I gave him a blue slime for free and he was happy. He decided to keep on going but take his time and in the future he was going to make his own comic books. I told him "Zain, you gotta get the money first and make sure they sign their name on the receipt and give them a delivery date." I told him to be aware of his customers' likes and wants.

**Business Tip #5: Always make sure the customers prepay for their orders or give you a small deposit because they may change their minds and your hard work and time is valuable!**

Dear Unicorn Friend,

I just organized my entire room, and now my baby brother is playing with my doll accessories and just ran away with my baby sunglasses. I'm looking back at all my success and I'm looking forward to the new year! I have been experimenting—brainstorming all the things that I like and my customers like and thinking about how I can combine them into one. Everyone loves slime and a lot of kids are looking forward to the new stuff. Maybe I can make a kit that comes with all the supplies which will include many colors and involve creativity and learning. I'm doing my research I'm trying to figure out what my customers LOVE and WHY! Kids need to live their life too and have the things on their wish list. I'm going to start by creating a survey with ten questions for my hundreds of peers at school so I can create the most amazing, mind blowing, breath-taking invention ever. Calling all ages, all genders, all backgrounds introducing my amazing product. It's going to be flying off the shelves, and it's all going to start with one simple household ingredient….baking soda. Paris here I come; Alayna Ffrench "Slime Queen" coming through!

Stay Tuned…

# Chapter Nine: Reinventing Your Products

Yesterday, my amazing mother and personal assistant ordered me some business cards, custom stickers with a princess holding a cupcake and a wand, a custom pen, mouse pad, and custom T-shirt with my "Slime Queen" logo on it plus my email information and such. This is really exciting because any business owner knows you gotta be ready for an opportunity, ready to promote and advertise your products and/or services. I can't wait to get them they will be delivered in two weeks, just in time for Valentine's Day! I am also getting ready to add Valentine's themed slime to my product list. I am going to include mini red and white heart beads or charms. This slime is going to be a nice light pink with an amazing strawberry scent which is sure to get my customers in the Valentine's spirit. I decided to package my slime in mini plastic bags with a tight seal and my new business card stapled to the top. I also have stickers to put on the plastic wrapping to add to the outside of the slime bag which is going to make my slime stand out.

### Dear Unicorn Friend,

I was thinking I really miss my cousins; they live far away. We used to play with squishies and we played with slimes and I can't wait to go to London to see them. My cousins Shanaya and Taliah always helped me restock my slime products; they are very helpful. Hopefully I can convince my mom to go visit there soon as I have business to attend to with my cousins. We are going to start our own Slime Club where we get all of our friends together, we have a party and make slime, make videos about slime, and experiment with different slime recipes. One day I will own my very own Slime Shop; I can picture it now.

I just ordered some more unicorn stickers to add to my packaging and bought a bulk pack of beads, charms, foam beads, different glitters, and mini slime accessories. I have to keep thriving and coming up with new and exciting ideas for my eager customers. I'm thinking of using clay to make unicorn charms. My calendar is full with exciting upcoming events including Valentine's Day, my tenth birthday, and a two day student entrepreneur event where students get to showcase their products for sale. This event is taking place at my school and oh yeah, it's on, for real, no doubt. All proceeds go to charity which is amazing.

When I came to this new school in September, I sparked ideas and led my peers to be inspired by my business talents. Some kids would come up to me and say "Oh Alayna you have competition, other students are taking your business" I replied, "No it's okay if they're trying to become entrepreneurs." I like everyone to be successful and take part, advertising themselves. It actually helps me learn and be self-reflective on my strengths. My peers have really great ideas and I look at this as an opportunity for growth and networking.

**Business Tip #6: Networking is a piece of unicorn cake. Telling friends and family about your business can help you get more sales and interest in your product. You can also learn from the success of others just by starting a conversation.**

No matter what, you should always follow your dreams, and try to stay positive. What's the point of getting mad and angry? If you want something bad enough, I believe one day you will make it happen. I never thought I would ever have my slime business because I never had the supplies and I doubted my friends would ever be interested or like my creations. I never thought my mom would help me as much as she did, but she knows I am very persistent. No matter what I find a path and a way to get where I want to be in life. You can't change who you are for anyone and I always embrace my true self. I know that I will always find a way too and my goals are to share and inspire others. I appreciate all of the help and support because it means the world to me. Thank Mom!

As crazy as it seems, my friends are obsessed with slime and my business is very successful. Tonight I'm going to restock my orders, make some copies of my new Valentine's flyers, hug my mom, eat some Caesar salad, go to the dollar store to buy some glitter, and get some cute ideas for packaging. It's freezing outside but my customers are depending on me.

My grandpa opened up a savings account for me so when I need supplies, I just take it out of my account but when I make sales at the end of the week, I deposit the earnings back into my account! Currently I have $300; not too bad for a nine-year-old business woman LOL.

**Dear Unicorn Friend,**

Life is hectic. Valentine's Day is around the corner and I'm barely ready to go. The clock is ticking, I need to produce slime and produce it now, I have twenty orders to fill in three days, OMG!!!! HELP!!!!

Later that night. I packed my lunch, ate some unicorn rainbow cookies and magical milk, and drifted off to bed. I was excited and nervous all at the same time, but as a professional I have learned a lot throughout my journey from networking to dealing with customers and handling cash to formulating cool packaging ideas.

Guess what girls and boys? Valentine's Day had finally arrived. I woke up early at 7 a.m. to get all my orders in order. "Time to make that cash, and add it to my stash, I'll sell it so fast, it's gone in a flash," I said to myself. LOL I like making up lil rhymes and songs in my head.

**Business Tip #7: Holidays are a great way to sell extra products especially if they can be incorporated into the theme, like Valentine's Day slime that's pink and glittery.**

So I'm at school walking through the doors the bell rings. As I looked to my left and see my reflection, I felt good about myself for making it this far. My teacher saw me and complimented my outfit, once again. She says, "I like your

*Alayna Ffrench*

cute outfit Alayna," and I said "Thank you very much, you look great as well." There's no better feeling than getting a compliment, especially from your teacher. I decided to wear red and black tights with a red sweater and a cute red headband to match with hearts on it. I'm also wearing my lil heart diamond earrings. So glam!

*Dear Unicorn Friend,*

Today at school I brought some of my leftover Valentine's Day slimes and some other slimes I've made in the past. I have two customers who are buying slime on Monday, still building my clientele, but my new Valentine's Day flyers will definitely spark interest and increase my sales.

# Chapter Ten: Never Judge a Book by Its Cover (but My Cover Is Pretty Awesome)

So there's this boy Johnny at my school. He seems to always be looking at my products and is always very curious and wants slime but never has money to order any. He tries to get slime for free and I am always saying no. But then one day I figured out that he wasn't stalking me as I suspected. He was just very curious about being an entrepreneur and wanted to learn how it works. Johnny, in fact, was trying to be creative and learn from me. I was inspiring him, and I didn't even realize it. Johnny figured that by understanding how I was networking and socializing that he could perhaps learn from my techniques.

Alayna Ffrench

**Business tip #8: Don't judge a book by its cover. Always give people advice and help them succeed, and always help to boost their confidence level.**

So I helped him and gave him advice. I asked Johnny what kind of business he wanted to start, and what kind of things he was interested in. After that we became friends but not just any friends: entrepreneur friends.

Dear Unicorn Friend,

Today was soooo busy. I just came home from school looked through my chest, added up all my sales and orders, and realized I had made a total of $110. I knew with my mind-blowing Valentine's Day flyers, my slimes would go viral and would sell like hot cakes. I feel so above the world, like I just won a million medals. That's what succeeding and making my own business feels like to me. I will always live life and achieve my dreams. Today, I made a promise to myself to **never** give up and always look on the bright side.

Valentine's Day is my third favorite holiday, after Christmas and my birthday, of course. At school we were allowed to eat gum and candy all day. There were so many treats like cookies, cupcakes, chocolates and Valentine's Day cards. I also sold my slime which everyone loved because I had so many different types, like pink and white beads, hieroglyphic glitters, and 3D glitters. They loved the cute packaging with the two heart printed ribbons on the side and heart printed clear plastic bag.

We each donated $1 to participate in gum day which is a fundraising effort to help the school. Today I had gym and I blocked a bunch of shots in basketball, oh yeah I'm the best.

After school I was sitting in my room and I had an idea to use my pink fluffy yarn to knit cute heart-shaped mini pillows. I got pink, white, and red construction paper and cut out some hearts out then decorated them with pom poms and glitter with some ribbon. I'm going to make these sweet keepsake gifts for my family members because I want to show them how much I care and appreciate them. Valentine's Day is about love after all. My daily routine for today also included baking some vanilla cupcakes with red sprinkles inside then layering it with red icing. I also sprinkled some confetti sprinkles on top which were white, red, and pink. At night when I can't sleep I pull out my Paris fashion pillow that conveniently has a pocket on the back which is where I keep my pen and pad to sketch out my ideas for my future fashion enterprise. Because today is Valentine's Day and I'm in a red mood. I am designing dresses that are red with some pink and white hearts with a cute satchel belt that is lined is white with fluffy arms. This dress comes with a cute white bow to match and the high heels are cute white and to top it off a cute fluffy purse, white with red hearts and pink flowers.

So tonight I was just relaxing and trying to restock my slimes when my baby brother Malachi comes in my well organized room and messes it up. He then goes and takes my baby alive bottle ugh. So I go and ask him where he put it and he doesn't know. After he finally remembers where he put my baby alive bottle, he leads me to it and hands it to me. He is very smart and intelligent so I think he just didn't feel like getting my baby alive bottle. Then I fed Malachi some yogurt (like two containers) and he still wants more. I'm thinking this would make him content and happy so I can get back to work but boy was I soo wrong. When I said "No more," Malachi started to freak out and throw a big tantrum. Because he keeps on eating all the yogurt in the fridge we had to buy a new fridge lock and I keep it locked and now he's even more mad.

I decided to take a break from working and teach Malachi my calming routine. I turned on my fake candle, put some calming ocean music on the computer, and laid out my yoga mat which is very long and purple. My baby brother Malachi copies my every move and tries to do my yoga stretches and meditate lol. After yoga we watch some funny videos on my tablet, and after about 10 minutes Malachi stretches his arms and shuts his eyes and falls asleep.

Well Unicorn friend,

It's been fun. Another year is almost gone! Wow time goes by so fast when you're busy and having fun. Tomorrow is my 10th birthday party and I'm going to celebrate it in London with my cousins Shanaya and Taliah and of course my big family. What do I want for my birthday? HMMM let me think well I would love a cell phone so I can make important business calls, and I can save all my important contacts, do a daily blog, make mini slime videos, and make lots of beautiful memories. I also want a gift card to the mall, and last but not least I want to get my nails done at the nail salon.

When I was at school today, I felt like I was in a dream because when I was walking down the hallway after first break, I heard the words "Slime Queen" in the distance and my ears were instantly shocked. As I got closer to my classroom all the students were calling me "Slime Queen" and everyone was staring at me with big smiles. It's like they were all proud of me because of how far I've come at my new school this year. I felt like I inspired many of my peers to be better and to try something new. I was almost in tears because I couldn't believe how many people actually cared and how much I made a difference with my slime passion. Alayna Ffrench AKA "Slime Queen." Well I will ttyl I gotta pack my cute outfits for my trip to London for my next adventure.

Life as a ten year old is just beginning.... Stay tuned for my new exciting journey of a 10-year-old entrepreneur.

- Alayna Ffrench signing out(:

# Survey:

1. What is your favourite type of slime?
2. Have you ever made slime?
3. Have you ever had your own business?
4. If you could start your own business what would it be?
5. In what way does my story inspire you?
6. Have you ever experienced any challenges at school with peers?
7. Explain your inner cookie mold (personality)
8. What is your most creative idea?
9. What should I write about in my next book?
10. Do you like unicorns?
11. What's your best piece of advice for me?
12. What is your favourite part of the book?

**Thank you for completing this survey!**

Please send survey and fan mail to:
Alayna Ffrench P.O. Box

CPSIA information can be obtained
at www.ICGtesting.com
Printed in the USA
LVHW071245260120
644822LV00017B/1245